Colores: amarillo
Colors: Yellow

Esther Sarfatti

Rourke
Publishing LLC
Vero Beach, Florida 32964

www.rourkepublishing.com

PHOTO CREDITS: © Nicole S. Young: title page; © Viorika Prikhodko: page 3; © Renee Brady: page 9; © Thomas Gordon: page 11; © Eric Isselée: page 13; © Tim Starkey: page 15; © Elena Aliaga: page 17; © Ariusz Nawrockis: page 19; © Marcelo Wain : page 21; © Jaroslaw Wojcik, Marcelo Wain: page 23.

Editor: Robert Stengard-Olliges

Cover design by Nicola Stratford, bdpublishing.com

Library of Congress Cataloging-in-Publication Data

Sarfatti, Esther.
  Colors : yellow / Esther Sarfatti.
    p. cm. -- (Concepts)
  ISBN 978-1-60044-520-0 (Hardcover)
  ISBN 978-1-60044-661-0 (Softcover)
  1. Colors--Juvenile literature. 2. Red--Juvenile literature. I. Title.
  QC495.5.S358 2008
  535.6--dc22
                            2007014033

Printed in the USA

CG/CG

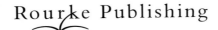

Rourke Publishing

www.rourkepublishing.com – rourke@rourkepublishing.com
Post Office Box 3328, Vero Beach, FL 32964

Esta página es amarilla.
This page is yellow.

El amarillo es mi
color favorito.

Yellow is my favorite color.

5

Me gustan las flores amarillas.

I like yellow flowers.

Me gusta la pintura amarilla.

I like yellow paint.

9

Me gustan los autobuses amarillos.

I like yellow school buses.

SCHOOL BUS

11

Me gustan los
pájaros amarillos.

I like yellow birds.

13

Me gustan los
baldes amarillos.

I like yellow buckets.

Me gusta el maíz amarillo.

I like yellow corn.

Me gustan los
polluelos amarillos.

I like yellow chicks.

Me gustan los
lápices amarillos.

I like yellow pencils.

21

Hay muchas cosas amarillas.
¿Te gusta el
amarillo también?

So many things are yellow.
Do you like yellow, too?

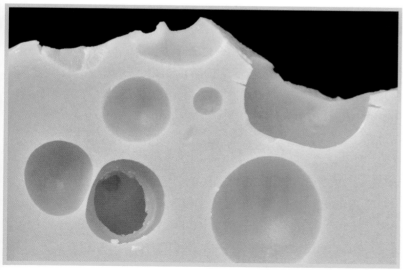

23

Índice

Index

Lecturas adicionales / Further Reading

Anderson, Moira, Finding Colors: *Yellow*. Heinemann, 2005.
Schuette, Sarah L. *Yellow: Seeing Yellow All Around Us*.
  Capstone Press, 2006.

Páginas Web recomendadas / Recommended Websites

www.enchantedlearning.com/colors/yellow.shtml

Acerca de la autora / About the Author

Esther Sarfatti lleva más de 15 años trabajando con libros infantiles como editora y traductora. Ésta es su primera serie como autora. Nacida en Brooklyn, Nueva York, donde creció en una familia trilingüe, Esther vive actualmente en Madrid, España, con su esposo y su hijo.

Esther Sarfatti has worked with children's books for over 15 years as an editor and translator. This is her first series as an author. Born in Brooklyn, New York, and brought up in a trilingual home, Esther currently lives with her husband and son in Madrid, Spain.